Kids Celebrate the Alphabet

TOTLINE® **BOOKS**
Warren Publishing House, Inc.

Warren Publishing House, Inc., P.O. Box 2250, Everett, WA 98203, 1-800-334-4769.

Printed in Hong Kong
First Edition   10 9 8 7 6 5 4 3 2 1

Library of Congress Cataloging-in-Publication Data

Warren, Jean, 1940-
     Kids celebrate the alphabet / by Jean Warren: illustrated by Teresa Walsh—1st ed.
         p.   cm.
     "Totline books."
     Summary: Includes an alphabet rhyme as well as art and science activities related to letters and letter recognition and song ideas.
     ISBN 1-57029-162-4

     1. English language—Alphabet—Juvenile literature.
(1. Alphabet.) I. Walsh, Teresa, ill. II. Title.
PE1155.W27 1996
428.1—dc20
(E)   95-22197
                                              CIP
                                              AC

Warren Publishing House, Inc. would like to acknowledge the following activity contributors:

Diane Himplemann, Ringwood, IL
Marie Wheeler, Tacoma, WA

Kids Celebrate the Alphabet

By Jean Warren

Illustrated by Teresa Walsh

A is for alligator, airplane, and ants.
A is for astronaut doing a dance.

B is for ball and block and bee.
B is for baby waving at me.

C is for crayons, car, and cat.
C is for clown in a funny striped hat.

D is for dinosaur, doctor, and doll.
D is for dog, who comes when I call.

E is for envelope, editor, and egg.
E is for elephant with four big legs.

F is for flag and fish and fox.
F is for firefighter wearing red socks.

eee

fff

G is for glasses, grapes, and goose.
G is for goat, who is on the loose.

H is for horn and hearts and hat.
H is for horse I love to pat.

I is for ice cream, igloo, and ink.
I is for ice skater dressed in pink.

J is for jack-in-the-box, jellybeans, and Jeep.
J is for janitor, who loves to sweep.

K is for kangaroo, kite, and king.
K is for kittens, who jump at string.

L is for lobster, ladybug, and lamb.
L is for lollipop I hold in my hand.

kkk

M is for monkey, mask, and mouse.
M is for moon high over my house.

N is for necklace, necktie, and nest.
N is for nurse, who makes patients rest.

mmm

nnn

O is for octopus, overalls, and owl.
O is for orange I eat with a towel.

P is for pizza, parrot, and pig.
P is for puppet that dances a jig.

Q is for quarter, queen, and quail.
Q is for quilt I bought at a sale.

R is for roller skates, rainbow, and raccoon.
R is for rocket that flies to the moon.

S is for soccer, scissors, and star.
S is for skier, who likes to ski far.

T is for telephone, turtle, and train.
T is for tulips that love the spring rain.

U is for umbrella and underwear.
U is for umpire, who has to be fair.

V is for violin, vest, and vet.
V is for violets I love to get.

W is for wagon, watch, and wheel.
W is for watermelon to eat with a meal.

X is for x-ray and xylophone.
Y is for yodeler yodeling alone.
Z is for zebra and zookeeper, too.

Now our alphabet rhyme is through.

Xx Yy Zz

Alphabet Songs

A Is for Apple

Sung to: *"The ABC Song"*

A is for apple, B is for ball,
C is for candy, D is for doll.

E is for elephant, F is for frog,
G is for goose, H is for hog.

I is for igloo, J is for jam,
K is for key, L is for lamb.

M is for monkey, N is for nail,
O is for owl, P is for pail.

Q is for queen, R is for rose,
S is for scissors, T is for toes.

U is for umbrella, V is for vase,
W is for wind blowing on my face.

X is for x-ray, Y is for you,
Z is for zebra in the zoo.

Marie Wheeler

A, B, C

Sung to: *"Three Blind Mice"*

A, B, C; A, B, C.
Sing with me—A, B, C.
A is for apples we love to eat,
B is for boots that we wear on our feet,
C is for candy that tastes so sweet.
A, B, C; A, B, C.

Elizabeth McKinnon

Alphabet Art

Masking Tape Letters

Use masking tape to form letters on sheets of white construction paper. Let your children sponge-paint all over the papers. When the paint has dried, have the children peel off the masking tape to reveal the unpainted letter shapes.

Decorated Letters

Cut a large letter shape out of posterboard. Set out glue and pictures of objects that begin with that letter (ants and apples for *A*, bats and bugs for *B*, cats and carrots for *C*, etc.). Or set out stickers or rubber stamps showing things that begin with the letter. Let your children decorate their letter with the magazine pictures, stickers, or rubber stamps.

Letter Books

Make a book for each of your children by stapling together several pieces of white paper and a construction paper cover. Print "My Letter Book" and a child's name on the front of each book. On each page of each child's book, print a letter that is contained in his or her name and then set out magazine pictures of things that represent those letters. Also set out upper- and lowercase letters from ads or article titles. Let your children choose some pictures and letters and glue them on their book pages. Then let them "read" their books to you.

Alphabet Learning Fun

Alphabet Accordion Book

Fold 13, large index cards in half and tape them together end-to-end. (Tape both sides of the cards for a more durable book.) Label the sections of the cards from *A* to *Z*. On each section glue a small picture of something whose name begins with the letter that is printed on it. Fold the cards together accordion style. Let your children have fun "reading" the book to you or to each other.

Alpha-Match Puzzles

Use 8-by-10-inch posterboard rectangles to make puzzles for the letters of the alphabet. To make each puzzle, cut a rectangle into three puzzle pieces. Use a felt tip marker to print an uppercase letter on the left-hand piece and a matching lowercase letter on the right-hand piece. On the middle piece draw a picture of something whose name begins with the printed letter. Set out the pieces of several puzzles at a time and let your children have fun putting them together.

Alphabet Mail Game

Make mailboxes by covering the lids of three shoeboxes with construction paper and cutting a slot in each lid. Put the lids on the boxes. Print a different uppercase letter on each of three index cards and tape them to the backs of the mailboxes so that they stand above the lids. For each mailbox, print a matching upper- or lowercase letter on the fronts of five sealed envelopes. Then mix up the envelopes and let your children take turns "mailing" them through the slots in the mailboxes, matching the letters. Make new envelopes to review different letters.

Letter Hopscotch

Use chalk to make a hopscotch game-board on a sidewalk outdoors (or use masking tape to make a gameboard on the floor). Print a different alphabet letter in each square. Let your children take turns hopping or stepping from one square to the next. As they do so, have them name the letters in the squares.

Alphabet Sticks

Turn a shoebox upside down and cut two parallel rows of five slots in the top. Gather ten tongue depressors. On five of the tongue depressors print different uppercase letters. On the other five tongue depressors, print corresponding lowercase letters. Insert one set of tongue depressors in one row of slots. Then let your children insert corresponding letters from the second set in the appropriate slots in the other row.

Alphabet Wheel

Cut a 12-inch circle out of posterboard. Divide the circle into eight sections and print a different uppercase letter in each section of the wheel. Write corresponding lowercase letters on eight clothespins. Let your children clip the clothespins around the edge of the wheel on the matching sections.

Alphabet Cooking

Alphabet Breadsticks

Use a package of frozen bread dough to make breadsticks in the shapes of alphabet letters. Follow the baking directions on the package. Do some of the activities listed below before enjoying the breadstick letters for a snack.

- Place the breadsticks on a tray and have your children name the letters.
- Let each child select a breadstick from a tray and name the letter.
- Make breadsticks using the beginning letters of your children's names. Have each child select the letter that begins his or her name.
- Use the breadsticks to spell out simple words.
- Make pairs of letters. Place them on a serving tray and let your children find the pairs.

Alphabet Soup

Prepare your favorite canned alphabet soup. Do some of the activities listed below before enjoying the soup for a meal or a snack.

- Have your children look into their soup bowls and point to letters that they recognize, or letters in their names.
- Ask your children to look into their soup bowls and try to find pairs of letters.
- Name a letter and ask your children to try to find it in their soup.
- Show your children the soup can. Ask them to name any letters they recognize on the can.